When God Has Been Called Away
To Greater Things

First published in 2010 by
The Dedalus Press
13 Moyclare Road
Baldoyle
Dublin 13
Ireland

www.dedaluspress.com

Editor: Pat Boran

ISBN 978 1 906614 32 4

Dedalus Press titles are represented in North America by
Syracuse University Press, Inc., 621 Skytop Road,
Suite 110, Syracuse, New York 13244,
and in the UK by
Central Books, 99 Wallis Road, London E9 5LN

Cover image © Bekir Gürgen / iStockphoto.com

The Dedalus Press receives financial assistance from
The Arts Council / An Chomhairle Ealaíon

When God Has Been Called Away
To Greater Things

Grace Wells

DEDALUS PRESS
DUBLIN, IRELAND

ACKNOWLEDGEMENTS

Acknowledgements and thanks are due to the editors of the following magazines and periodicals in which some of these poems, or versions of them, first appeared:
Contrary Magazine, Crannog, Galway Whatson Broadsheet, Kilkenny Poetry Broadsheet, Poetry Ireland Review, Sharp Review, South Tipp Today, Southword, Succour, The Kilkenny People, The SHOp, The Stinging Fly, The Stony Thursday Book, Windows Authors & Artists Introductions Series Magazine and *Wildeside Magazine.*

Poems have also been included in the following anthologies: *Landing Places: Immigrant Poets in Ireland,* edited by Eva Bourke & Borbála Faragó, Dedalus Press (2010); *The Echoing Years: An Anthology of Poetry from Canada & Ireland,* edited by John Ennis, Randall Maggs & Stephanie McKenzie, published by the Centre for Newfoundland & Labrador Studies, School of Humanities Publications, Waterford Institute of Technology.

The author would like to extend her sincere thanks to Kilkenny County Council whose Writer in Residence appointment generated a number of these poems, and to South Tipperary County Council whose Artist Bursary enabled their editing and completion.

For Richard, Sliabh and Holly
and for my brother Henry

Contents

THE NEW LIFE

IN SUCH A CITY

LOVE IN ALL ITS FORMS

Osborne's Animals

JIMMY: We'll be together in our bear's cave, and our squirrel's drey, and we'll live on honey, and nuts—lots and lots of nuts. And we'll sing songs about ourselves— about warm trees and snug caves, and lying in the sun. And you'll keep those big eyes on my fur, and help me keep my claws in order, because I'm a bit of a soppy, scruffy sort of a bear.
      —*Look Back in Anger*, John Osborne

It wasn't bears and squirrels with us
but bears and bears.

I, who had been raised in a family of mice,

in my twenties a beau
whose world was inhabited by mongers,
I shared their space
not knowing exactly what they were, or where they lurked.

I can't say I minded or disapproved—
not of the mongers, or the mice or the bears.
I'll take make-believe and fancy,
I'll play *Let's pretend*

as we stumble forward
half-formed, ursine,
deeper into the territory
of becoming.

Somewhere on Barnes Common
A Box of Chocolates

The boys who rode into our Eden were rough,
we had the sense not to give them our addresses—
bad enough they'd found our favourite tree

where all summer we'd sprawled like lionesses
uncaring of any world below,
afternoons spent in serious talk of what awaited,

only to jump back onto our bikes, to speed
from the future's clasp, dodging the Common's
scrubby bushes, defying gravity, inviolate.

Their leader took a shine to me, and persisted,
shaking us from branch to earth, so we'd arrive
to find them, languid as panthers, in our place.

Cast out we had no choice but to let them in,
though all was changed: we shared a Common tongue.
He brought me chocolates in a sealed box,

I would have dared their dark shell, bit eager teeth
into the sweet, white flesh, only my sister
said he'd stolen them. She banked on fear, threatened

the police, insisted the evidence be thrown away.
I leant upon the wisdom of her age, half-sensed
a jealous hiss behind her care. No matter that I didn't eat

them then, nor how far my young arm threw that box,
distance couldn't shield me; the contents bore my name,
kisses, betrayals, desire's complications: love in all its forms.

Adrienne Wants Due Regard for Home-making

after the sculpture 'Escape from the kitchen'
by Maria Griffith

Today I saw a troika of shallow, wooden crates:

they might once have held sprouting potatoes
or penny packets of seed tied in rubber bands.

Stapled across one crate, a cooling tray for baking
boxed things off like the grille of a cage.

Behind it a pestle for pounding herbs and a paddle
for slapping dairy produce into shape.

From the wire hung an implement for carving butter,
yet sharp and strange enough

for procedures on the body, a forgotten cure
for hysteria, the vapours or *nerves.*

In the second frame the soft hair of a pastry brush
contrasted with the rigidity of an icing cone,

while a steel sieve—fixed at a jaunty angle—
harvested all manner of silent wisdom.

There was a darning mushroom, the last bead of an abacus
and other objects whose purpose seemed obscure.

It was all wood and metal, and spoke
of our mothers and their mothers before them.

In the last box, yarn stretched like the strings of a harp
and wooden spoons were gathered in a stand,

the whole so laden with resonance it positively sang.

Bequest

In this book I leave my mother's shopping lists
and my grandmother's ration coupons

and the letter her husband sent her from the camp,
emptied, marked with a swastika
and the words OPENED BY CENSOR.

I was never sure what to do with it until now,
nor with the handwritten note on the back which read

my most treasured possession
an envelope from a brave man.

The Coat

Her mother's face said it was a brown and shabby thing,
second-hand and quite beneath them.

Her father mumbled there'd been something similar
in his youth, lost with the years.

Sisters admired it, but wouldn't try it on;
brothers borrowed it, left it out in the rain.

Friends were never sure what to think,
tried not to be seen with it in public.

Lovers stowed it in the wardrobe depths,
during quarrels attacked it with their knives.

But she danced in it with her children,
let their tiny hands stroke the wondrous cloth.

Time came when she wore it everyday,
slept in it, woke each morning fully clothed.

In the Legend of this Moment

Even at the distance of an aisle—bottled water, soft drinks—
though doubt and distance hold off greeting, I know it's you.

Even at the distance of an aisle there's our split-second arc
of recognition—two Princes chasing the one stag.

Only the play of your life intervenes, small sons clamour
boisterous demand, your needle wife stabs at shopping.

I am too far away to salute you, too remote to stop this drama
escalating in its crescendo of domestic strife.

I would put out my eyes to save you the pain of witness,
but still glide toward your disaster and when I'm close enough

for your name on my lips—you dive into the depths of the trolley,
a sudden, vital scramble in groceries, elbows knifing me away.

In the legend of this moment, being Pwyll, Prince of Dyfed,
I would grant you a year and a day in my own kingdom,

and taking up your guise, travel to your world to slay all that ails you.
Doors to Otherworlds being closed, I'm left to pass by, within ice
    whispering

Dig on, scrabble in your pit, that which your fingers rake
is what kill you, and make your stories strong.

Nightwork

Even asleep I try to make honey from your bees,
my progress one small drop on the dresser
where my mother kept her precious things,
silk scarves and scent and leather goods
opened only by my sister and me, in secret,
whilst you brought her swarms
and allergy, a sticky trail
of frames, boxes, hives and winter sugar
boiled in its spilling pan,
inviting wasps to dim our windows,
ants to cross her kitchen floor.

Choking on the cooked scent of wax
and wax itself filling her cupboard space,
she cursed your bees
and they died, hive by hive
of your old age and Veroa.
Strange then that they should live on,
scuttling, swarming panicked dreams,
fueling my tireless attempt
to make something of their sting.

The Hostage Place

Invisible, the insect held within the amber of our father's boat.
Hull he built himself, condensing his finest fibres into boards
that bore the lick of sun and wave until their taught wood sang.

Evening light could strike its umber sail to flame, light a vision
that denied the bite of rope, of salt, the angry sting, for, though
the rudder steered, our father drove with a lashing tongue. And

I never wanted to feel the look upon my mother's face upon my own.
That horizon gaze which stared beyond and saw nothing
left each of us unable to find a course out from his dark hold.

Each of us still able to inhabit the place we'd crawl; that prow locker,
cupboard for pump and bailer, anchor, and metal chain that clinked
into each wave, where to the kind sound of water receiving wood

we learned to sleep,
cheeks pressed into the life vest's sweating, yellow flesh.

Closure

There is always a door closing, a final out-of-here,
gone-from-your-life moment, the disappearance

of closeness, the togetherness shared
separated, parted, final.

Through a door rapidly diminishing footsteps
bruise our softness, only for it all to lessen

and deaden with each step, until at last
a gulf so wide they are gone, never to be seen again.

And years go by. There is news, a marriage,
a child, a career, a death. Or no news—

they walk away down the plank of a hall
to step off into nothing, to disappear without trace,

continuing that step-by-step away from you,
only to never really leave, so wherever it is they end up,

or roost in the arms of fate, they continue
to walk the body. Sometimes whispering

in the forgotten reaches of our extremities;
on occasion, stumbling through the briars of dreams

to leave on the tongue in the morning a kiss, or burn,
to shadow slip out of and back into a crowd,

recognised momentarily on a stranger's face,
before they walk on, walk away, keep walking

deeper into the marrow of our bones.

The Funeral Director's Wife

Often I have watched his hands about a corpse,
the closing of the mouth like the closing of a tin can
gaping and wide; the jagged edge of memory
prevents a smoothing over.
He will conquer death, make of it a business
dressed in ceremony; his chiselled face
sets more stone-like with the years.

He doesn't know I sit with them.

The talk in whispers is of first kisses,
the way a loved one's lips turned sour in argument.
We share trinkets, baby hair kept tied in ribbon, flowers pressed
between the leaves of faint-ink letters
from sisters gone over the Atlantic at seventeen.
There is the telling of waking alone to the dark night
and of the shamings, teachers and fathers,
and I hold them, hold their passing, hold the dearest of things

while in the scrubbed yard he reverses the hearse.

The Dress

for David Donohue who told the story

Remember how poor we were? The wolf curled
so tight at our door we tripped on it daily
until the stumble became a soft brush against fur, manageable,
its teeth a snarl of threat that never harmed
as if it had grown used to us, was glad
of the small scraps we threw from our table.

The children brought their own light,
steady as the glow of nightlamp burning
by bunk-beds. We were blessed;
quiet, curious—there was much of you in them—
and you got down beside them
to share their games.

What was left between us was thin, but fine
like the silk of the dress, so when we saw
it that winter, we recognised its cloth.
The street silent, dark but for the lit window
drawing us like moths. You saying,
It was made for you. And it was.

Black folds swung to the knee. Scalloped shoulders.
The waist tailored to my own. A bodice
low enough to frame pale skin, breasts, beating heart;
I burned to wear it, Christmas coming
and my wardrobe shabby. Still I pulled you away,
Don't be daft, I'd never have the occasion.

It called into our dreams, crying down small lanes.
We heard it and couldn't sleep and bickered:
I burned food, dropped things, snapped at the children.
Even the wolf grew restless. Our soft days tarnished
until the relief when I saw it gone, lifted
from bare window, leaving me fit back into my life.

But what did you go without, sacrifice, bargain,
to make them wrap it in ribbon: you
who didn't have the money, nor I the occasion?
Still it looked well about me when its time came
and I stood shaking hands, accepting condolences,
offering the children small comfort,
as they lowered you into the earth.

Priory Lane

for Liz

Your destiny was not a house but a road,
the long approach between the golf course
and the walls of the asylum, the way
the cars swore past, their noise violent
to our secrets, so you had to shout
techniques for kissing and dreams for the weekend,
Saturday's trawl for clothes, parties to be crashed.
Enough time for confidences, your father's fury
and your mother's alcohol and still we didn't reach
the end of the golf course, nor break
the monotony of the asylum wall.

Aches in our legs, shoulders drooping we moaned,
How can you walk so far twice a day,
how can your parents be so mean?
The trucks raced on, the pavement droned like the teachers
who promised failure. It was so far to the house
where you hid from his wrath and his belt
we rarely accepted your invitations,
so you walked Priory Lane alone.
Was it any wonder where it led you—
you who had learned early, how one foot
in front of the other, will always take you away.

THE PRINCESS AND THE FOX

The Princess and the Fox

Every dream I'd ever had was out for airing the afternoon he came.
We left without them, save the bridal dress.
The qualities I saw in him that day never waned
yet grew overshadowed by the sharpness of his teeth,
the scent of blood about the jaw. I hid myself
in his animal grace, loved the fineness of his coat, its bright flame.
We shared a quality of oneness, in time scorched black
by our surrender to his longing.
A scorching I later found to be necessary;
through its fire I came to all that remains immutable.

She would come only so far willingly,
there had to be some use of force.
Things were easier after the scene in the forest;
there was less confusion as regards her perfection and my wanting.
Afterwards she rode my back with an air of resignation,
but her knees still held their passion, a music that haunted me.
They sang a tune I would have followed
to the far corners of the known world. In the end
she left without forgiveness. I understood. I had taken her
to the last abyss, where the accursed may yet become sacred.

Horse Fair

Their child and marriage barely a year old,
she pushes the pram amid horseflank and sinew,
a waltz of colt and foal, piebald and skewbald, roan
and bay, hooves skittish, laden with threat.

The lens of her camera too narrow
for the full scene, not swift enough
to capture the moment
bargains are sealed. Her focus

returning always to the one man
who'll grin for her and pose. He walks
the fair green at her back, setting the pace
until she becomes the herded; driven.

Later the town streets among stalls
of cheap trinkets, the fingers of vendors,
the shadow of touts and hawkers.
Slowly she'll understand he belongs,

a man who'd sell his grandmother, sell his wife.

The Only Medicine

What's left, when the father of your children
has thrown a basket at you, hard,
upturned the kitchen table
breaking all the china you possess?
Driven off into the night? His absence
clothing the house and the children
as they struggle with the buttons on pyjamas
and your thoughts are of leaving
but you don't leave,
you don't go anywhere.
They love him, want the two of you
to be together,
and that
seems more important than everything else.

The only medicine is words,
to write it all down,
to say how that desperate blue bottle
lands so accurately between the eyes,
to record the butterfly
that flaps trapped in the lampshade, the way
you share this house with nature
or she shares it with you,
as if grass would start growing
between the floorboards.
And the world is in chaos
and their father is a violent man
and tomorrow, tomorrow, tomorrow
your daughter is two years old.

Tableau

for Tess Morrissey

First you will come upon your neighbour on the lane,
beneath elder blossom, above meadowsweet,
creamy hedges lining the way as if to a wedding;
aisles decked with ragged robin and loosestrife.

You will throw your arms around one another,
your broken heart breaking in the look upon her face,
you will cling and weep and say goodbye.
You are leaving the russet dog and the black kittens.

You have snapped roots to rip yourself from this ground.
No time for your roses, no matter their hunger
for your lips in spring: at your feet are suitcases
and small children scattered amid them.

But everything is going to be well. You will
take the all-day coach, board the ferry at midnight.
The city and its empty pockets await you,
just as the taxi driver comes now to take your bag.

He is packing the trunk of the cab, he is driving
you away. Years later, thinking on those rounded
shoulders, the veined hands at the wheel,
you will see the great fold of wings beneath ordinary clothes.

Rescue

In silence I'll descend the mountain road.
They'll not hear the gate or the lift of the latch
as I enter the black cottage where the only light
is her own dimmed glow. But I know my way, know
he is there to the left watching the film she has begged
him not to show. Any moment, the scene
where the football jock holds the head
of that woman beneath the pool
because she won't suck his cock under water.

And I can feel the water tear the lining of her nose,
taste it in her mouth, its throb fill her lungs,
so the gasp that echoes down the years as she finally
bursts the surface, might be my own. I can still see
her crawl from the edge, but I'll leave that actress
limp away, for it is not her I have come to rescue,
not her I have come to rescue but my own self, hunted
to the bedroom shadows. The children curled in cots

and no sanctuary except that last crouched corner
of the house in the hole she burrows for herself
by the floor, quaking, beyond tears, her mouth,
her lungs, her penis-choked throat denied air.
What can I say to her? A ghost-self I have no tongue.
I hover, extend my arms, the poems, images
of the grown, safe children. Scoured of faith
she will not believe, I offer her blind eyes the world,
but nothing will let her rise from this moment,
only that I stretch out my hand, lay it
on her head, on the short stubble of her hair.

Clearing

In winter I started, in those sparse days of low light.
I went to the back of the back field, hidden, hiding, and I began.

Ivy filleted the brambles. Elder grew awry, hawthorn
hobbled, root bound, fumbling over the tumbled wall.

Bracken encroached on the hill, spalted and matted, spare
and sparse and brown. It was January,

I was writing of the dark things he'd done; mornings
begun with the tongue sealed to the roof of my mouth.

I prized free an old rose, overgrown, snarled up, thorned.
I trod the green of unseen bluebells back into the ground;

debris by the armload and sheep at my back, eating the dark
leaves where they fell and I didn't think of cock and cunt

and the strings he pulled to move my puppet hands.
It was thorn and thicket, briar on briar till the loppers broke

snapped blade blunt in the bound knot of stem, ivy trussing trees
that wept and called out and no one heard

when I cried in the mornings, in the small room
we called the studio, sun pouring through the windows,

my white tissues heaping like snow. I wasn't just weeping.
I spat. Rocking on my heels, fists at my eyes and on them

the scars of blackberry vines sewn through the old hedgerow,
thrust deep, binding tighter, over, under, over

an impossible maze, impenetrable forest: undefeatable creature.
I cut and pulled, reeling wires of briar behind me, piling,

walling myself in, then sifting it all again, forking back and forth
over the field, building a bonfire higher than a man.

I was deranged. Time against me. The days short and new months
falling fast, so I was driven, pursued. The red fox

of ambition never far off. I didn't know it would take a year,
a whole year. The cured hedgerows leafed and emptied,

the black pool of fire's scar grown over before I'd write
the last word, close those covers,
walk once more into the shimmering world.

Renaissance Portrait

for Maire Kinsella

Lend me Carpaccio, better yet Crivelli,
grant me a Renaissance Master to paint all this.

Does it matter what I'm wearing,
the room he paints us in, or the view?
Only that we're caught, hung
immobile in a thick, gilt frame:

my rogue knight with his enigmatic expression
that dominates the scene; me simpering,
naive, the hem of my cloak lined
with ermine, symbol of purity.

I would have made a good Madonna,
our trauma equal to the Annunciation,
the ride to Bethlehem, the old refusal at the inn—
not to mention everything that came later.

I begin to understand her mask of forgiveness,
the way it can be pasted to a face,
lips tamed. The only trouble is the eyes,
hard to know what they betray.

But all that's no matter. They were hard times.
Others belong in this portrait: solicitors,
a judge. Those officials
in the colours of the duchy are social workers,

the woman looking on with such compassion
is my counsellor. Pale hands hold open a book.
There ought to be a white flower,
an owl winging the dark,

so long as there's an apple for original sin,
a braying ass to anticipate the apocalypse;
ruins depicting the inability
of some to see the true light.

At our feet a green snake threads a skull
to warn of life's transitory nature;
the artful arrangement of a cucumber
suggests rebirth; and two lizards

emerge from hibernation
to allude to the resurrection of Christ.

PIONEER

Pioneer

The last memories of her husband have been sewn
into a quilt which barely warms her nights.
After bad dreams, their son and daughter sleep
furled beneath small flags of nightshirt
and brushed cotton sleeve worn thin.
Four summers and their harsh winters
have passed since she marked his grave.
Her own parents write, begging her home,
begging, before the children run quite wild.
Formally, they offer a second cousin
with land near York, ask she seriously consider
this most suitable widower of some renown.
Their letters go unanswered.

She is loosely moored between two worlds,
anchored only by the children,
for all they have ever drunk is from the well of this place.
And what flows in her now
is rainwater, woodsmoke, silence reflected
on the lake surface; leaves turned,
hair snagged on briars. Stones. The small,
white feathers that line nests.
She is sung with fox bark and pheasant call.
Creatures roost in her thoughts, her days
are measured by the slink, the leap, the pounce,
the pitched balance of wings breaking into flight.
She too moves in feral ways.

And lavender soap on Sundays is a fine gauze veil.
Though the men in church stare with downcast eyes,
she knows what it is they smell on her, and, wary of hunters,
is afraid. She lives where the long road from town
meets the trackless purple mountains. Some nights
leaning into the silver shadows at her door
she wonders who will come for her first.
For the quiet is also pregnant with alcohol and laughter,
with a swagger some miles off, and there are eyes
that watch from the mauve shadow inland;
if she stood still long enough,
had she interest in belonging,
they would take her as one of their own tribe.

All she has carved for herself is a small square of land,
free of chickweed and scutch-grass, soil abundant with seed.

When She Speaks with the Children

she speaks of childish things,
silence pressed on her so long
the tongue has been stilled.

Thoughts smoulder in her.
Were she really to speak again,
she is no longer sure
how her voice would sound.

A strange cry. Not bird song.
Perhaps like the dog fox barking,
neither musical, nor sweet,
more a rasping howl

toward the ineffable crowded
at her door, hung in the branches
about her house,
ripe for harvest.

The Lone Parent Does Not Write

Between a bad back
and a deadweight Hoover
it's been a month or more.
Let's not talk about the duvet cover
walking out of the bedroom
in search of a good home.
At the sink I'm breeding botulism—
a resistance experiment.
Results are good,
besides, my kids have more brains
than to get sick; if their mother
stopped this frantic whirl
to tend a fevered brow,
she'd keel over, replace them in the bed.

This morning allows
I find our rooms again,
vacuum the top of rugs at least,
nothing too fancy,
nothing extreme.
This way I'm left
a tiny sacred hour,
to climb the laundry mountain
to part the sea of toys
and walk through,
the Egyptians at my back,
to sit,
for just one hour, here
in the Holy Land.

Go, My Thought, on Golden Wings

for my mother and my father

The September we drive to Normandy
he's six months dead. For you, a break
from the weeks of probate law, a full stop
to your years of nursing, to his long decline:
the hospital's pyjamas and indecencies,
only you there for the hours they left him in corridors,
only you when he rolled from gurney to lino
and your arms not strong enough
to catch the weight of such a man,
yet the pair of us so used to it
we carry him through every mile of Normandy.

How it rains, all the world's weeping washing France
of every speck of Summer dust, robbing the children
of sand-castles and picnics, sending us indoors
to every small attraction the place can offer.
In the subterranean room of the *Maison de la Mer*
caged fish swim absently, vast eels hide,
coiled in crannies, everything second-hand, inglorious,
turtles groping in their gloomy bath—
junk shop of the nautical,
and only your grandchildren come alive
stroking the flat wings of flat fish.

After the fifth day of rain, children, mothers,
the ghosted empty plains of Caen,
we drive forty miles, circle the city,
battle its motorway, pass orchards
of industrial estates, villages sawn in half by roads,

finally turning onto the 'cidre route'
as if we were Alice, gone through a small door
to find apple trees, white cows, idyllic farmhouses,
the rain painting a watercolour,
fields pleaching into one another,
all of it drowned in the children's boredom.

For them we visit France's largest model railway,
where our passionate guide recites a litany
of train type and track length before disappearing
beneath the layout to emerge high in the Alps,
like God in the heavens. At his command
windmills turn, boats steam into harbour
and the tiny wheels of tiny trains turn over tracks,
to speed from stations, past schools and churches,
their carriages crossing the bridges of fast-flowing rivers
tunnelling the papier mâché mountains
as they hurry between the proud, old towns of Europe.

Then gradually the lamps dim; a chorus of Verdi rises.
We stand in the darkness of the Chemin de Fer bewitched.
Each small window has its lamp, candles flicker behind glass.
All through the miniature night passengers board punctual trains.
He would have loved it here. The music swells,
allows us to believe that the innocent are sleeping safe
and those who brought us through that last great war
are not this minute spilling from hospital trolleys
to hospital floors, that every thing is timed, scheduled.
That it all makes sense. That we are watched over.
And all our small lives are glorious.

The Death Slide

for Silvia

Always you dragging me to the wild edge,
salt-splattered, windswept days at the sea,
the centre of peat-dark lakes curved
in the belly of mountains. The heart of things.

You again, December, your daughter's birthday,
evening dark against swimming pool windows,
the earth at her furthest tilt,
our hopes moths battering the glass.

Shepherding a flock of small bodies in towels
and bathing hats, you part waves with a strong hand,
and steering us away from the past you insist
we mount the steps of the Death Slide.

Fearful tunnels, water in the mouth and throat,
until we're spilled frothing into each other's arms.
Over and over we climb the steps, repeat the precious
moment of looking one another in the face,

eyes shinning before the flight. And I know
this is how it will be one day, the two of us
at the top, our last goodbyes,
the spinning darkness, the meeting again on the other side.

Pelvis

And what is it made of? You choose.
Silk has always been suitable. Sometimes wood.
There are women who beat copper, smelt bronze.

Coal has certain precise qualities; even salt. I knew a woman
who made hers all of fruit. Another chose feathers
sparrow and pheasant, the speckled breast of a thrush.

I've seen girls steal from peacocks, witnessed the sewing
of a thousand rhinestones: some love that jazz, that razzmatazz,
to sculpt themselves from a slick sax solo in the night.

Mine, I filled with water from the mountain stream,
washed it—strange how the water
muddied and curdled and cleared.

I dried it with sphagnum moss, polished
till the moon shone on bone.
I came up lovely, good as new.

True, it took time to clean out the old images.
I was old before I was done.
But a woman doesn't loose herself with age;

she deepens, keeps changing:
mother-of-pearl, alabaster, china clay.

Muezzin's Call

Crossing the Suir at Ferryhouse,
passing the frosted orchards,
a sound in the throat rises—
resonating voice of the land.

Passing the red acacia, this ululation
sweetens to a note. Passing the holly
red with berries, passing the hotel entrance,
aware they hear me, the health-club visitors,

the chambermaids, the waking sleepers,
past the last yellow leaves of the fingered
birches, past the woman
whose face has caved in with sadness,

beneath the only mistletoe for thirty miles,
over the Gashouse Bridge, through
the November morning I go, one note
rising up and out of me over the town,

calling the world to prayer.

When God Has Been Called Away
To Greater Things

Much of this life you have been alone and lonely.
The wolf no longer howling in emptiness,
your heart a rusted camp bed, prized open.

Some nights God lies down there.
God says, *This mattress is very thin.*
God says, *There is little comfort here.*

God sleeps there anyway. In the morning,
when God has been called away to greater things,
the bed is rumpled. There is an imprint, which lingers.

My Garden and Those Who Made It

On a day in September I heard its voice,
not the calling out of duties and need,
the hundred tasks, but a song
like a stream below ground;
Remember how I was? Impenetrable,
a briar forest worthy of fairy tale.

Nettles armoured against all comers,
a mined stretch of glass, bin-liners,
drink cans, scrape of pickle and jam in jars,
rags of cellophane strewn between sodden nappies
and ashes from some ghosted hearth.
I hauled all that away.

Then the clearing of brambles,
like a person cropping grass with scissors.
Clippers, secateurs, and gloves that were never
thick enough, or grew too damp
and frail and gave up before I advanced a yard.
Cutting back to reveal builders' rubble,

stone, cement, the branches of a fallen tree;
one wild gooseberry the only treasure.
I piled and burned and burned and piled.
One day my neighbour found me, our talk
all of the weather, of the price of things,
and back he came half an hour later

with strimmer and petrol because he'd not
seen anything *modern*. We worked for an hour,
Seamus cutting and clearing, revealing
more space than all my weeks had,
yet even then I saw my days
of following men and machines were over.

Finally stretching black plastic which lifted
and flapped, blew off onto spikes, tearing holes.
Rain ran in rivers off it or puddled above rats
that burrowed and nested and at last a day
when digging began: a strip as wide as my arm
through the debris of a fallen wall.

Like ploughing a field with a silver spoon.
It was inch by inch until Tom came.
Tom with his bad nerves and his forking up
the water pipe, cutting it in two.
Tom breaking my tools, nearly setting fire
to the house; *Wretched Tom,* I called him.

And Georgia Billingsley the Third,
who dug beside me and told
of hills in Northern California
cut for housing estates, and of her time
at the border, helping to feed those ready
to risk their lives to reach America.

How she had befriended a boy who aimed
to hitch seven hundred miles to find his father.
So in the earth beneath my elder tree
the ghost of that child remains, buried
with the hope that a child of eleven
could traverse a continent and find one man.

Before St Patrick's day, I planted potatoes there.
They cropped with such abundance,
I could only weep.
Into the broken hills of California I sowed
parsnip and beet, parsley and broad bean.
Poppies grew of their own accord.

Then Chmielnicki came. I set him
to the impossible root tangle the earth had taken
thirty years to knit. He took his fleece off
in my garden in the spring light
and his body in that blue vest was what?
A nation's flag, a national anthem,

something you reach out to no matter what.
I joined him prying earth from its binds,
my own soil needing be more friable.
He tried to bring me to science and I him to *Spirit*.
The theory of relativity was water off a duck's back,
Why would you want to square anything anyway?

But he knocked at my door one night
and I let him in. He knew so little of love
I think God was looking for someone
to teach him. All summer I tried to fit his plan,
played chess, listened to facts and figures
until I became incapable of clear thought.

I rebelled, taught Chmielnicki something he didn't know
of numbers: that a woman can begin the summer
with a boy of twenty-six, end it in the arms
of a man of sixty-two. God said, *Teach him about love.*
I broke his heart. But a garden forgives.
Sweet peas fragile as butterflies blossom,

roses bloom, bluebells multiply along the ditch,
the magnolia the children gave grows strong.
In autumn you grub in bulbs brown
as chestnuts, small, dull-looking,
you are lighting a taper that in the fullness
of time will explode your sky.

A garden forgives everything. You stand back amazed.
October comes with its cold and damp,
the sorrowful wilt ushers in despair—
enough to stop the heart. Before your eyes
the garden climbs up onto the cross, surrenders
perfect limbs to the rope, to the nails,

dies back to reveal the Christ-being within.

Sign

'Duty is the most sublime word in the English language,'
—General Robert E. Lee

Your words white birds breaking free
from the cupped palms of a defended heart;
message of duty furled beneath breast feathers—
they knew their flight exactly.

As if long ago we'd agreed.
As if we'd said,
Let them be our sign.

Had we been told
you were being sent to the South,
land of defeat, heroism, Lee?

Did I entreat you to keep them safe,
knowing by the time we met
I would have undergone the burning,

at my hips a skirt of black wings, charred
fragments and, within, skeletal ghosts
of tumbler and fantail stirring the moted air.

But who could have known it would be August,
beneath prayer flags of fuchsia,
in the bright light of montbretia,
this invitation to the new life?

THE NEW LIFE

For Everything Which is Infinite

In Halloween dusk we came. Small witches had gathered in the campo by the church of Mary of the Miracles. Mist reigned in the lagoon. We moved into blue November's gilt mosaic, bowed by the Byzantine, humbled before icons. A decade in Europe's last dark place had put out my eyes. I had forgotten beauty.

You led the way, Torcello, Carpaccio, Bellini—each tile a glint on the path. You gliding us down the Grand Canal: the Gritti Palace, the white marble of the Guggenheim. Slick, black gondolas teaming turquoise water. You, birthing me back to life.

My task was to navigate our thoroughfare, our moth-flutter at windows, the weave through merchandise, diamante and velvet, shot-silk and brocade, our studious pauses with book-sellers; I pulled us on, in, deeper into the old maze.

Let me live here, I prayed, in these streets: my own flowers by the door, laughter and wine and work, someone practising the piano in a room nearby. *Let me live here*, I said and let go your hand to find my future street. I could have walked forever, beguiled, inwardly singing; charting the labyrinth; in the heart of it paused beneath a lit window: a woman's smile, the fan of cards, a hand drawing out the ace.

The New Life

i. *It Begins when the Leaves Turn*

She tied the blushed bohreen leaves. Faced north.
Took stock. Heard summer end in the thrum
of small creatures at harvest, in flickering
wing-borne hearts deciding course mid-flight.

On darkening roads she would drive the scarlet car,
unravelling time, driving to meet him.

Days going out into her garden, fingers charted
each increasing blemish, mould spores, wilted stems.
She turned branches, put her lips to the small brown details
of decay. She owned the land, loved how winter

crept forward, took possession. How the promise
in its breath stirred her, frost lining each vermillion leaf.

ii. *February*

This time of year the gossip takes its own roads;
we dine on root vegetables and the marriages of others.

The Turkish reserve a separate tense
for matters not seen with their own eyes.
Here the white mouths of snowdrops open
to speak of my father's funeral. You,

who are so many miles from home, write
to soothe me. I see love travels faster than light.

iii. *Whenever We had Sheep in the Field, You Quoted Milton*

Milton at the breakfast table, Milton in my hat and gloves,
corn bucket in hand, crossing the frosted yard,

Milton mocking the clergy and their fold:
The silly sheep look up and are not fed.
His line circling my head, I'd purse my lips
and think on your arguments for education.

How I'd counter with the arts of life and loving.
Weren't we proof of their sovereignty?

The silly sheep look up and are not fed, and it was winter,
the scene soft brown, our field a wash
of mustard meadow, hazels dropped pale catkins,
siskins focused the landscape's yellowed theme.

Milton's time had come and gone, the sheep gorged
on our winter grass, we feasted on each other and were fed.

iv. *If I Owned a Dress*

I would wear it this night
coming to meet you from the evening train.

By it you would know I had set aside the axe and the saw,
firewood stacked, bookcase planed to silk.
I'll trade sandpaper for emery board, nails clean
in the half-light of the car where you lift my skirt;

the scent of frost-bright fields and the blue lingering descent
to dusk washed with the feral from my skin—
my fork and lift of brambles, briar forest I took these weeks
to clear, our acre reclaimed. Already I imagine primrose,
celandine, a bank of bluebell, meadow orchid.
Let me wear gardenia, I'll put your diamond on my hand.

Don't ask me to understand these mysteries,
to speak of wildness or explain the freedoms of tamed things.

v. *June Marriage*

This then is how it should be, June, hills rolling
to the distant world, heat rising from the greened earth.

Leading you back to our bed.
Celebrants before the hour of work.
At last coming to the page unkempt, alive
to your footfall in the yard, to birdsong.

So friends might call, make their way down the aisle
of our bohreen and finding us thus, bear witness.

Cartographies

It took my breath, your body with its scars,
their multitude dense as stars in January.
I'm just mapping you, I said, the ends of my fingers

charting conflicts whose ghosts shimmered
like restive Confederates on the grass battlefields
you would later take me to in Tennessee.

That first night a wound on your chest denied me
the place I've learned to lay my head.
Shyly you explained the welts beneath one shoulder

were from an old operation on the lungs—
though their scar suggested someone removing wings.
I'm just mapping you, I said.

All these years later you come to our door bruised,
forehead in plaster, a dent the size of a coin
narrowly missing one eye. I reach up to kiss,

to trace the new curve. The finger I once nearly
lost in a kitchen accident moves across your brow,
trespassing the boundaries of *what if.*

Our Table

Interminable heat and interminable speeches defined that party
but what cemented its legend
was a seating plan that placed us in the company of brokers,
agents, underwriters, loss adjusters
and their bondsman wives all chattering insurance.

And they, recognising your last name, inquired if you
weren't that famous actuary from New York.
All night we reached beneath white linen to squeeze each other's
sweated palms; not blessed with easy conversation,
we consoled ourselves with thoughts of that other Tillinghast,

in that other place, seated at the poets' table.

Aşure

Aşure is the Turkish name given to the last dessert Mrs. Noah
made before boarding the ark. Because she was emptying her
shelves one final time, it contains an amount of everything.

Let me grate almond for you this night.
While gulls wheel their floodlit vigil above the Blue Mosque
let me shred pistachio green as limes from the Bazar.
Let me rub coconut to powder. I will take raisins crated in Tarsos,
yellow sultanas by the handful.
Grant me the İznik bowl I forbade you buy,
for it alone could hold this night, this Aşure.

Let me empty these cupboards the way Mrs. Noah
emptied hers that last night before the rains came.
Baking powder, bicarbonate of soda, cream of tartar.
Clove against toothache, mint for digestion,
thimble of brandy to ease our grief.
The light is low in this room. Soft brown
sugar. Nutmeg. Scent of cinnamon on my skin.

I will rasp orange rind, stir a syrup
thick with corn flour, arrowroot, gellatine;
cut an apple sideways to reveal its star.
Mrs. Noah took chick peas, the last rice, last
scrape of pearl barley, so who would notice
the salt from these tears? Let them fall
as I beat egg white, whip cream, fold in flour.

Jet bead of currant, maron glacés, crystal ginger,
nothing too good for this night, this Aşure,
so if there is a wail, a keen in the mouth
tart as lemon, let it be the morning call to prayer,

for they are laying you in the best sheets, my love,
your boat is leaving, everything ship-shape
and ready, every last thing prepared.

IN SUCH A CITY

Directive Ireland 2000-2010

after Robert Frost

Slip the constant stream of cars and take the old road south.
Best to go on foot, better it be raining. Let your feet again
know dust, mud, the matter of earth. Lean into the wet bank,
to the green band of hedgerow which as you walk reveals
herb Robert's spark, a glint of trefoil, the slow, intimate grammar
of growing things whose language becomes your tongue,
so that as you reach the dusk hills to climb amid rhododendrons
green and jungular, your mouth is a flower that can brook no lies.

The slope that opens onto heather leads to a monastery
offering rest, a place that fed hundreds in the famine,
feeds you now and would provide a bed, dormitory-style,
had you the time. But you must press on, the weight
of the country's change pushing at your back,
and turning from the pressure you descend
to a breeze stung with the scents of a spreading city.

Stay south, fuchsia now in the hedge, fuchsia now *the* hedge.
You will come to small lanes and small fields,
a tang of seaweed, the sea's siren call reassuring you
this is the way, so when you come to the harbour
and the boat waiting, you'll know to board. Humbled
by the ocean, the salt spray breaking on your mind,
you'll find the patience to reach in time—
too long a time to make this crossing easy—the island waiting.

Land beneath your feet, navigate the harbour path
and you will come to a gable end,
a ruined shop, and reaching up blind fingers
into the hole that is there, stretch for the coin
a boy and his father placed there summers ago,
and turning its silver in your palm you'll feel the salmon
of this country leap between the circle of your hands.

Woman Riding on a Cock

after the painting 'Clockwork Cockeral' by Desmond Shortt

It was the Old Testament that spoiled us. The springing
of water from stone. The appearance of flaming plants.
A parting of waves. We learned to expect miracles.
Now, we grow discontent with everyday wonders;
the flight of birds, salmon spawning upriver.
A bright moon in the day sky.

These things we take for granted. Breasts too.
Their shape and purpose.
The natural colour of hair. Laughter lines. The way
wrinkles age us, like the rings in trees.
These marvels are not enough. More is asked for. I acquiesce,
wander the desert, cut and tucked, striking rocks with a plastic staff.

For Every Doctor in Mozambique

For every doctor in Mozambique there are thirty three
    thousand people.
For every doctor in Mozambique there are thirty three
    thousand people

and never having been to that country I imagine
    their waiting rooms.
How every hundred miles or so
    there must be a vast atrium, all bright light

and fresh air like the central gallery of the British Museum,
    but larger—with enough good chairs
for the thirty thousand to comfortably, patiently
    wait their turn.

And because it has already been rather a long wait,
    some of the women have become adept
at delivering children, have developed breathing techniques
    and birthing postures that the pregnant mothers

employ without fuss, or drama
    so all that disturbs the patients as they wait
is the sound of newly born babies
    mewling prettily like kittens.

And because there are so many under-five-year-olds
    suffering from stunting and wasting,
the kind doctor provides a kitchen where all day
    they ladle bowls of porridge and soft brown sugar.

It must be said of those present, twenty percent
    suffer from AIDS, but there is great camaraderie

in the fact they are all in this together,
    adults, teenagers, infant children;

and though grandparents look on concerned, knowing
    they are about to loose a favourite son or daughter,
that it will fall to them to raise another seven or eight
    children on less than one dollar a day,

they take consolation in the nurses handing round
    lollipops and storybooks, and in the knowledge
that if they, or their grandchildren do succumb
    to malaria or tuberculosis, or malnutrition,

it will mean they can keep coming back
    to this beautiful room, to the cool air
on their faces, and the great glass ceiling.
    And though sixty-eight percent of them

do not have proper sanitation, they may at least
    use the doctor's lemon-scented washroom
with its automatic hand dryers and luxury soap.
    In those moments it is even possible

that their thoughts turn to us over here,
    to our medicine men with their
three hundred and fifty patients who come and go
    in estranged orbits rarely meeting,

while in Mozambique smiling orderlies are folding
    out camp-beds, fitting fine linen sheets,
plumping feather pillows; they know they have
    a long night ahead of them,

    the good doctor has plenty of people to see.

Table

By candlelight in the lap of canal water
on a street narrow as ribbon
they dine to the slow shuffle of passersby.

Do not stare, but the woman is weeping.
She holds small shields of hands to her face.
He is reaching toward her, a gesture of compassion,
but some dark source has put out her eyes.

Unthinkable in such a city!
Here palaces bow to the waters,
chandeliers burn to light the traveller's way.

Wings of angels stir to this table. White feathers
from the portraits of the Academia, cherubs
from a thousand ceilings. Gilt limbed Gabriel
and Michael loosen, lift from mosaic walls.

Even the lions are leaving their pedestals.
And shelves of hand-bound books lean to this moment,
profer their pages to drink her tears.

Plaster falls to show its pity. Stones stolen
from Constantinople mime empathy.
Doorknockers, cast as dolphins and goblins,
carol together, plainsong and love.

Consolation can not touch this woman; in her,
black convolvulus twines up
trumpeting the massed armies of misunderstanding.

Fear, ancient as that Atilla brought out of the Alps,
escapes through the cracks of the city,
for hers is a bloom on the bough
of darkness old as time.

He can do nothing but reach to touch her,
in time lead her gently from this place.
The white jackets of waiters move forward,

they brush down the crumbs, shake out a new cloth.
Here is clean silver, fresh china. Oil. Salt.
The same vase of flowers.
The two chairs, empty and waiting.

The Farm Stand

Such a crop of tomatoes! Such plump flesh, so red!
You walk them with pride to the stall at the end of your lane.
All summer you tended those plants, tied tresses, nipped buds,
talking to them all the while of harvest, never imagining such riches.
Place them in a basket you wove from the hedgerows, hazel
and willow and woodbine, beside tall jars of honey.
Again your hand will reach to turn its amber to the light
and you'll consider your bees, even the one
that comes now, drowsy with heat,
to bat at the roses you have bunched in their vase.
Remember the year you planted those roses?
As you dug the soil you were working on that song—
the one which made you all that money, that paid for your yacht
and the trip to Antigua, Tahiti, the Seychelles ….
Which was it? You forget, there have been so many.

The day is long. You are in no hurry.
Sit for a while in the Adirondack chair you crafted. Reminisce.
Rest your legs on your greenwood stool; think back
to the day you stumbled upon those ivy-twisted boughs,
carried them the miles home. It was long ago and autumn.
Now it is summer. You sigh for sheer pleasure,
the neighbour's child has just washed your new car, the coupé—
also owned by the Prince of Wales,
also driven by James Bond in his latest film.
It pulls a little to the left but you will have your man look it over.
Not now. Now your work is done.
You have collected a dozen eggs from beneath your chickens;
in the meadow your children and grandchildren gather wild garlic.
Familiar steps on the gravel behind you announce your wife.

She bears loaves of fresh-baked bread. Your wife; beautiful,
sensual. The woman who stood by you all these years,
who always listened, who gave good advice,
who understood your sense of humour. And your poetry.

Your wife. The one you would have married, granted that other life.

Threshold

for Nicolas Gehri

Come home. Home to your wife and child, to the taste
on the tongue of whatever it is you have planted.
To your shelves lined with music, books, to the voice
behind the bathroom door singing, to the washing up

not done, overdone, to someone yelling, the toilet roll
just finished, the bin to be emptied, the Hoover bag changed,
the needle on the record, to all you have created,
made space for, allowed in. Say yes to it,

yes with despair, with disgust, with longing for another life,
one you glimpsed today, one whose legs seemed
to go on for miles, one whose fitted kitchen was made of solid oak,
one whose Mercedes was parked outside.

Come home. Home with annoyance at the dust
under the stairs, the ring round the bath, the stain in the cloth,
the scar, the chip, the crack, the loose screw, the repairs
to be done, to be ignored; the restoration which may

or may not come. For all its abundance of crimes against you,
with their commonwealth of treasure stored in this temple
of condemnation and hope, for all that you have planted,
kneel here at the threshold of your life and kiss the ground.

In the Air Above Canada

Strange how these Atlantic flights to Chicago, Boston, Providence,
bring me to you, how Canada unfurled in folds
of black and white moraine beneath a fuselage, can bring me
over decades. Milk-white lake surfaces and frozen snow,

the miles stilled. From thirty-thousand feet no sign of life
now, nor in June 1943 when you came, twenty-one and ripe
with Hitler's war. On your face my brother's face, shadowed
by too-large a cap, Airforce greatcoat occluding narrow shoulders.

Only that last spring you had stacked tins in your mother's larder,
calculated audits in the city, kept an eye on Sheila Dean.
Your February diary records the movements of bees,
the direction of the wind, Churchill's advances and retreats.

Three German warships escape from Brest and steam through
the Straits of Dover. No cakes or sweets to be obtained anywhere.
I have your photographs, Number 31 RAF depot, Moncton;
barrack blocks. Rivers CNR station; refuelling aircraft.

Winnipeg, Manitoba, maintenance hangars, and winter Ontario.
Chapleau and Comox, seen from planes. You left me views
of and from Ansons: Crandall, Quebec and the Saskatchewan river.
Invasion of Sicily proceeds. Mussolini dismissed and Badoglio takes over.

Badoglio dissolves the Fascist Party. And then *Larry, Larkin, Tony,*
Bill Radcliff, Johnny Ross, The Baron—alias *Keith.*
David 'Cholmondeley' Owen, Flight Lieutenant Simpkins (Mr. Sim).
You called yourselves *The Skivers Union,*

posed on the beach at Point du Chêne in fashionable sunglasses,
in the arms of girls. You climbed each other's shoulders
one on three, on four, braced arms and stood firm.
Take girls home, say goodnight, over camp fence and into bed at 2 am.

Is it the black forests cut in their strange shearings,
the rough hills, the wide white expanses, or these lines—
roads, canals, rivers, railway tracks etched like graphic scars,
that suddenly make me love you?

Canada still offering its same views. Neither the pines,
nor the frozen lakes, nor the silhouette rocks forgetting—
not a history of battle dates and statistics, but the late
Larry Youens, killed in action 23rd of August 1944,

and A.J. Wallace lost in the October of that same year.
You left chalk notes, a cross above Barrett, a tick
beneath David, your young hand encircling *Billy* and *Trevor,*
underlining *Larry, Whiting, Tony*—your personal code.

Missing in action, died of injuries, lost at sea.
All unspoken, held and carried beneath your rage,
only to unfold in Canada, a landscape wide enough for grief.
Not alone the album you left behind, but Canada keeping

the memory of their lives. And though I consider
going down there, to seek out the descendents of those
who knew you as we never did, I know it's only here
in Canada's silent breath, my face pressed to the precious glass,

that I can slip through the monochrome to find
those young selves, the coloured world they left behind.

Halloween

for Holly

I baked. A whole day of it while blackcurrants
simmered, releasing their bloodied juice.
We'd already built a fire, hours
of gloved hands on damp timber stowed
beneath plastic till wood was ready for flame.

I carried blocks and planks for benches
and hefted out the grill. From
skeletal trees I hung a hundred
paper ghouls. It grew dark,
the girls lighting candles along the lane.

The moon rose and the wind dropped,
witches clambered from their parents' cars
and neighbours emerged
out of the black fields. The fire held
sending sparks into the darkness

and someone brought old fireworks
colouring the party blue. All night I
played host, tying bags
on the feet of those without wellies
handing round trays, food and wine,

walking back and forth from house to fire
for forgotten plates, the corkscrew,
marshmallows, toasting forks;
repeatedly fording the cold stream
as if it were the Styx

and for this one night I was able to transcend.
But I didn't labour so as to reach
something of the afterlife;
I worked to create that spooky beauty
for those of us on this side,

so against all the world's fear
my daughter and her coven could scream.

Pasiphae Speaks

Who was I to talk? All Crete knew my shame—
the woman who had mated with the bull.

Our progeny at the centre of the labyrinth,
I loved and feared my offspring.

Was any woman more tormented by her coupling?

And though I'd kept secrets from my daughter
she knew or guessed enough,

and would never come to me for advice.
What could I say to her when that bright suitor appeared

arrayed in the mantle of *the hero?*

That I had seen the harm in him
and knew he would betray her?

Some things are obvious from the start,
we do not escape our myths.

All Souls

Ambling back from the Halloween fire
I felt how good it was
to be free. To be drunk. To be loved.

The moon raced and lost to cloud,
a sorcery of silhouette hedgerows
held upright my homeward weave.

Bewitched, I no longer wanted to reach home,
instead a hunger to become
part of the ditch's intricate divinity,

I longed to dissolve into its pattern,
only vanity wouldn't let me
be a lone loosestrife or meadowsweet,

no delicate bluebell or vetch,
no solitary scabious or violet;
I had to be the song their totality made:

speedwell, daffodil, guelder,
dandelion, sorrel, dock,
hazel, chestnut, primrose,

eyebright, yarrow, self-heal,
willowherb, cherry, damson,
sycamore, spindle, skeogh.

There was so little in me that was humble,
one small white stitch of campion?
The rest was an orchestra, a riot,

nettle, hypericum, foxglove,
strawberry, celandine, pignut,
goutweed, woundwort, mint.

I wanted to heal all ills, to be
the mantle of the hedgerows,
all they stood for, all they were worth.

Yield

Annually the harvest is liable to be small,
three or four fruit much alike in shape and colour;
the hue of their skin, the taste in the mouth familiar.
Fruit of each season. Assuredly
one of melancholy. Mist. Departing swallows.

Something too of winter, of endurance.
Attempts to hold onto candlelight, firelight;
poignant moments, spare beauty.
Or more elusive: solidities—kindness,
spring quickening, summer's abundance.

And a slow seduction toward spring
which may in time produce fruit,
flawless, priceless, swelling
through a blessed summer of birdsong, dragonflies,
blooms opening, each more exact, more lovely than the last.

But whatever is done, whatever is achieved
it will only be the harvest,
many days of sunlight will have passed unrecorded.
How the rain that fell, or how the burn to young
leaves by bitter frost, was weathered, will not be known.

Just as the amount of dishes soaped
and cleaned that year will not be written down.
With time these things shimmer and dance,
now one leads now the other. The stick
once used to measure by stands idle against the wall.

For Silvia

While the carbon rose she was thinking
of the street where a boy she'd loved
had lived behind a low, black gate, its metal
on her fingers; her innocence and pain.

The thermometer reddened while she was dreaming
of a new dress, and the shoes to go with it,
the way she'd wear her hair, a man's hands
lacing pearls at her neck.

Islands began to drown as she was deciding
what to eat that night, something simple,
one of those meals you can pull together
from eggs, brown flour, a heel of cheese.

For some time she'd suspected things weren't right.
She changed her life. Cleaved herself to the land.
Planted trees. Raised a garden.

She bought a hive of bees, started to collect
rare breeds, two of every animal.
All winter she fed the wild birds.

She blamed herself for fiddling while Rome burned,
knew her every movement came too late,
all her small efforts wouldn't change a thing.

She tried on the whole wardrobe of despair,
a hair shirt of helplessness, scratching pullovers
of depression, the patchwork skirt of giving-in.

But she kept on scattering corn amongst her flocks,
keeping watch over her seedlings,
putting seeds into the ground.

When news came of panic in the streets,
the chaos of people swarming for lifeboats,
voices shouting, *Women and children first!*,

neighbours gathered to her hearth,
a man whispered it was like the Titanic going down;
the sound of her clear voice striking up a tune.

The Work

for Kerry Hardie

All day reclaiming the winter stream,
mud as dark as the spent black wood
which fouled its path. The stench
leaving an imprint beneath my skin.

Always this need to bring water
to its clearing, to free some withheld thing;
echoes of my mother and father enmeshed
in the root tangle of cress and waterweed.

Because patterns repeat themselves and I keep
thinking of you Kerry, over and again
attending to the metal of your being, polishing
its essence; turning yourself to find again

fingerprints to clear away. Evening
settling its blue mist on the November field
led me to leave down mud and boots and tools
at the door of the yellow-lit house, knowing

there will always be this work. Be trapped things.
Always that which flows seeking containment,
boundaries, ensnaring itself in the flounder
of longing and mistake making.

And it is the nature of elements that shine
to also tarnish, in the same way
that the expansive moon, which once more
silvers running water, will in time diminish;

yet I also know, you will leave here brighter than you came.

Lightning Source UK Ltd.
Milton Keynes UK
11 January 2011

165514UK00001B/14/P